FIRST TIME LEARNING
NUMBERS

Here's a short note for parents:

We recommend that you work through this book with your child, offering guidance and encouragement along the way.

Find a quiet place to sit, preferably at a table, and encourage your child to hold their pencil correctly.

Try to work at your child's pace and avoid spending too long on any one page or activity.

Most of all, emphasize the fun element of what you are doing and enjoy yourselves.

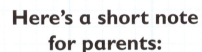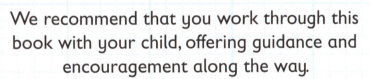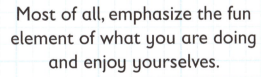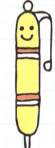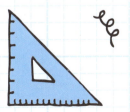

Birthday candles

Count the candles and draw a circle around the right numbers.

Birthday presents

Find a sticker of some presents.

Count the presents. Say the numbers out loud as you count.

More numbers

Find a sticker with two ducks.

Count the ducks and say the numbers.

Can you count from 1–10, then count all the way back again?

Quack, quack

Count the ducks and circle the right numbers.

Frog march

Find a sticker with two frogs.

Count the frogs. Say the numbers out loud as you count.

Number rhymes

Here are two number rhymes to sing.

1, 2, 3, 4, 5 once I caught a fish alive

1, 2, 3, 4, 5 once I caught a fish alive,
6, 7, 8, 9, 10 then I let it go again.
Why did you let it go?
Because it bit my finger so.
Which finger did it bite?
This little finger on the right!

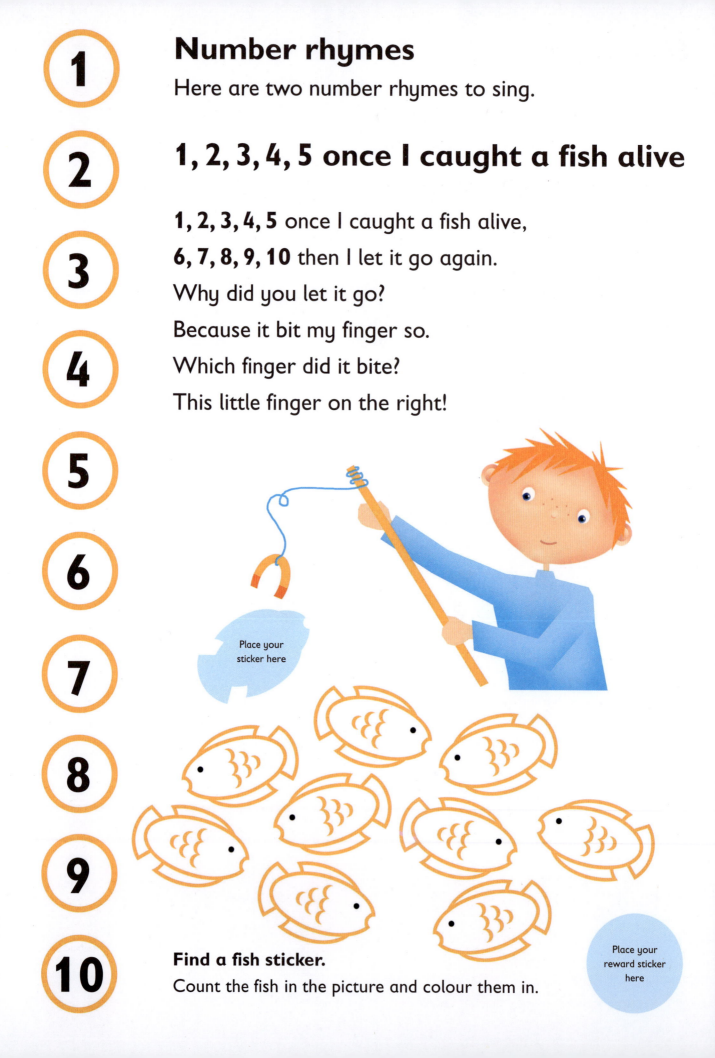

Find a fish sticker.
Count the fish in the picture and colour them in.

Sizzling sausages

Five fat sausages sizzling in a pan,
All of a sudden **one** went bang!
Four fat sausages sizzling in a pan,
All of a sudden **one** went bang!
Three fat sausages sizzling in a pan,
All of a sudden **one** went bang!
Two fat sausages sizzling in a pan,
All of a sudden **one** went bang!
One fat sausage sizzling in a pan,
All of a sudden **one** went bang!
Now there are no fat sausages sizzling in the pan!

Place your sticker here

Find a sausage sticker.
Count the sausages in the picture and colour them in.

Place your reward sticker here

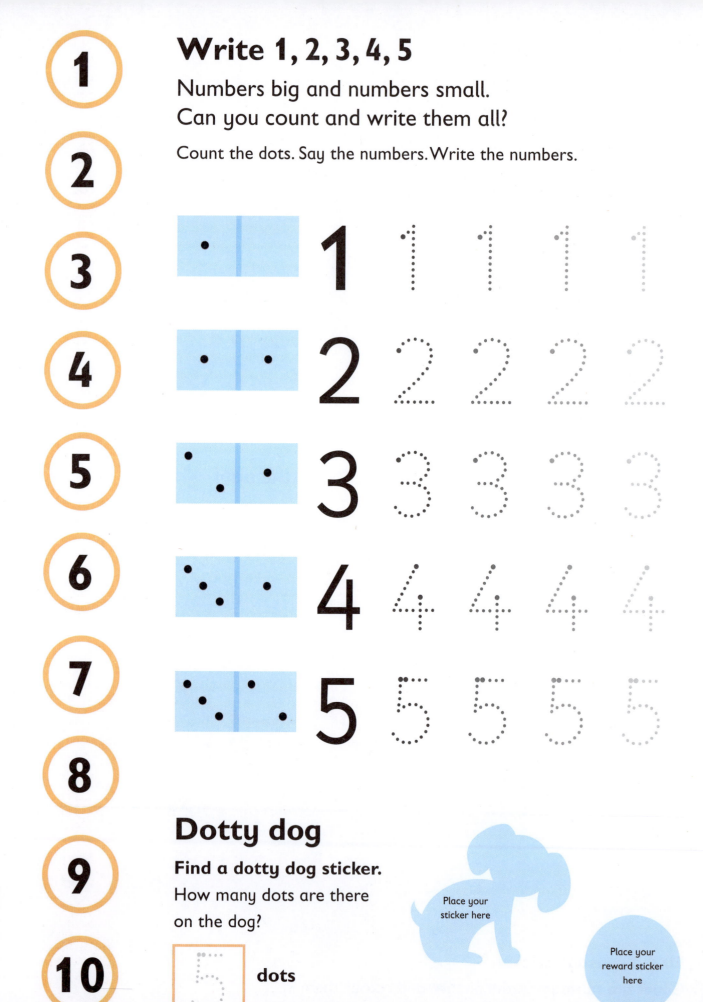

Write 6, 7, 8, 9, 10

Count the dots. Say the numbers. Write the numbers.

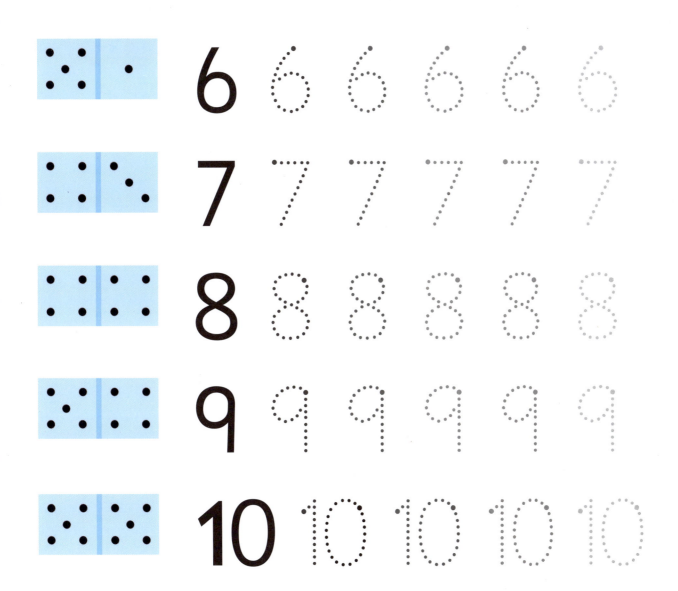

Spotty pig

Find a spotty pig sticker.
How many spots are there on the pig?

 spots

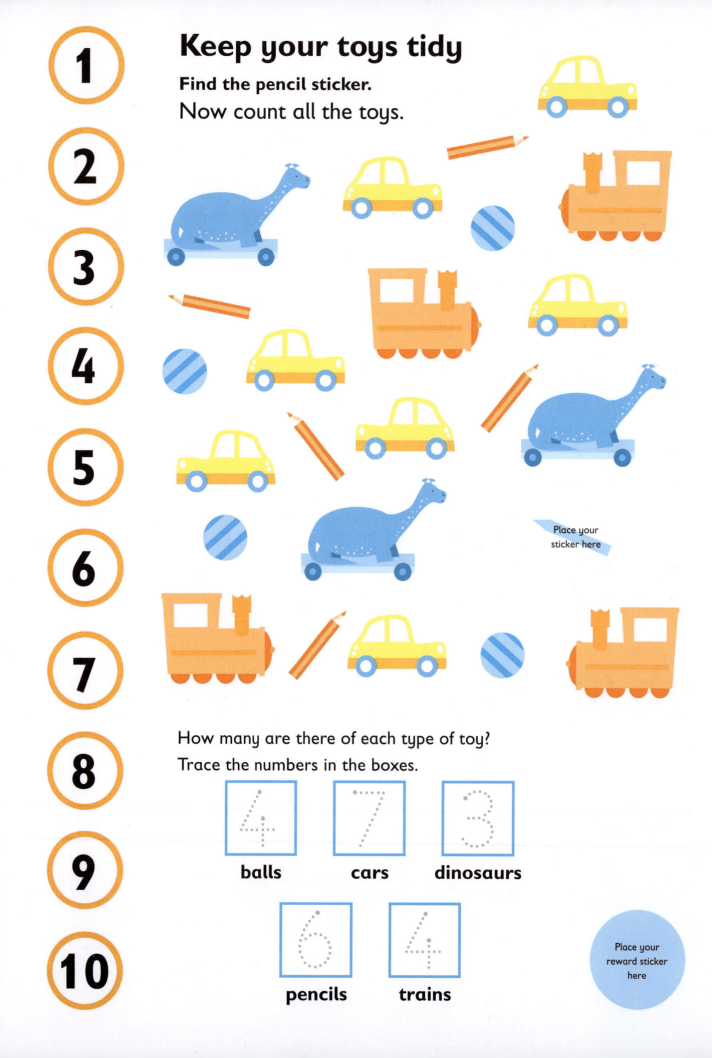

Paintbrushes and paint pots

Count the paintbrushes and trace the numbers in the boxes.

Counting toys

Count each group of toys. Draw a line between each group and the matching number.

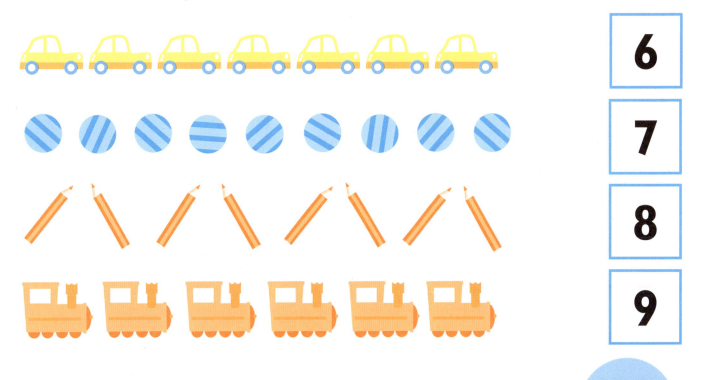

Place your reward sticker here

What's missing?

Write the missing number on the egg in each line.

5　○　7　8　9　10

○　6　7　8　9　10

5　6　7　○　9　10

Hoppity hop!

Count the hops the bird has made.

Find the number sticker that fits at the end of the row.

① ② ③ ④ ⑤   Place your sticker here

Count the hops and write the numbers.

① ○ ○ ○ ○   Place your reward sticker here

One more

Count the treats. Then draw one more.
Write how many there are now.

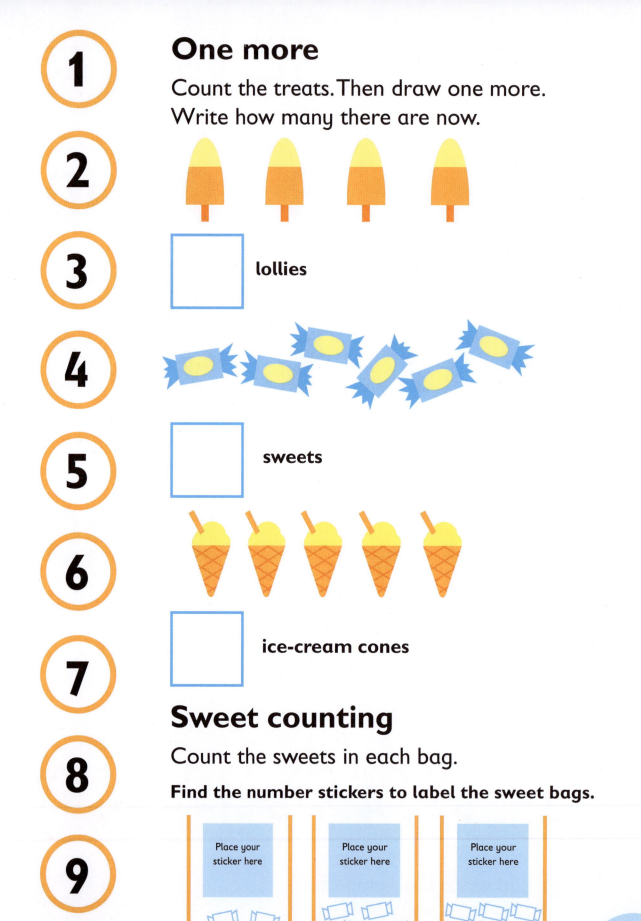

☐ lollies

☐ sweets

☐ ice-cream cones

Sweet counting

Count the sweets in each bag.

Find the number stickers to label the sweet bags.

Colour the bag with the most sweets.

One less

Cross out one thing in each line and write the number of things left.

Cup counting

Count the drinks on each tray and write the numbers in the boxes.

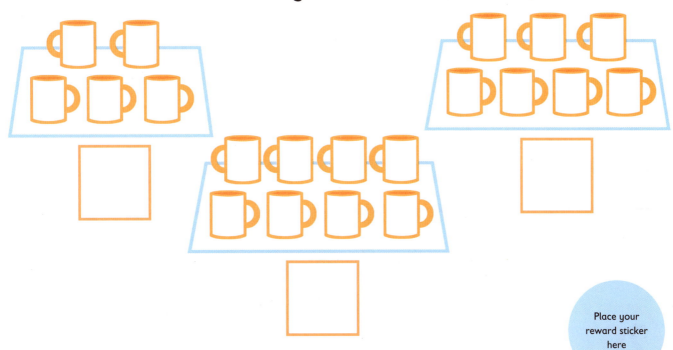

Colour the tray with the least drinks.

Place your reward sticker here

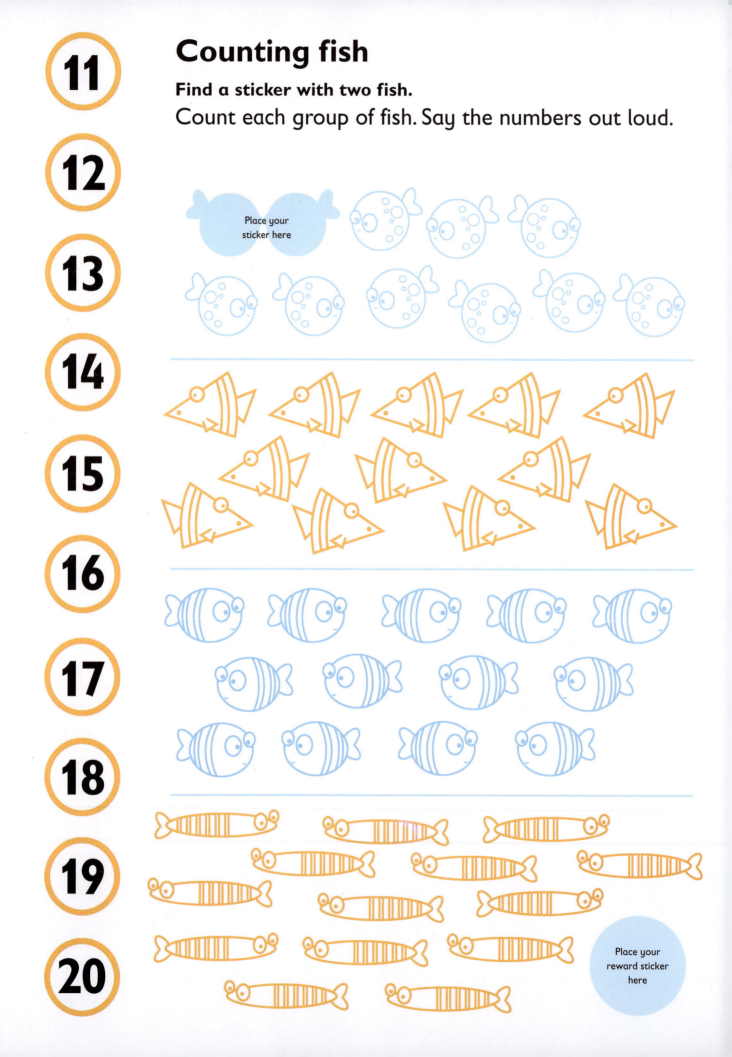

Counting fish

Find a sticker with two fish.

Count each group of fish. Say the numbers out loud.

Turtles

Count the turtles. Draw a circle around the number.

Starfish everywhere!

Count the starfish.

Find a sticker with more starfish.
Now count how many starfish there are altogether.
Did you count **15** starfish?

Flower show

Count the flowers. Trace the numbers on the vases.

Seedlings to grow

Count each group of seeds. Draw lines to match the seeds to the packets.

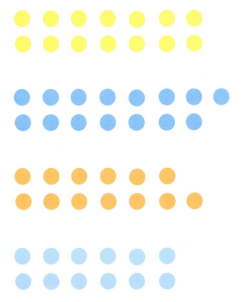

Place your reward sticker here

What's missing?

Write the missing number on the leaf in each line.

10 11  13 14

12 13 14 15

16  18 19 20

Hoppity hop!

Count the hops the frog has made.

Find the number sticker that fits at the end of the row.

1 2 3 4 5 6 7

8 9 10 11 12 Place your sticker here

Place your reward sticker here

Two by two

Find the missing sticker.
Draw lines to match each pair of animals.
How many animal pairs are there altogether?
Say the number out loud.

Two more

Draw **two** more items in each line. Count the cars and the cones. Write the numbers in the boxes.

cars

cones

Two less

Cross out **two** things in each line. Count the things left in each line. Write the number in the box.

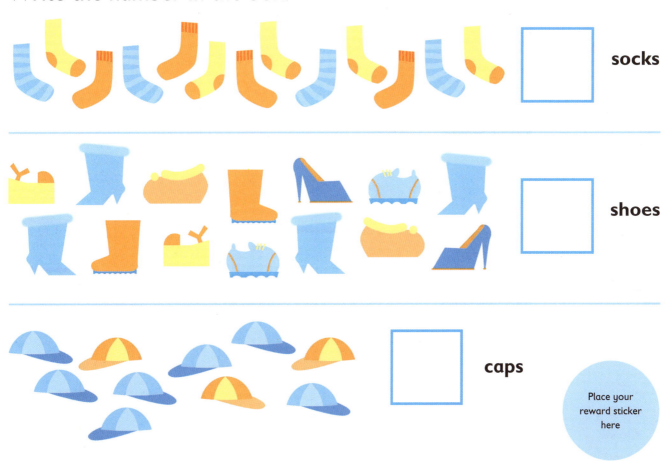

socks

shoes

caps

Place your reward sticker here

Hide and seek numbers

Numbers here, numbers there, numbers hiding everywhere!

Place your reward sticker here

The numbers **1** to **20** are in this picture.
Can you find them all? Colour in the picture.

15
16
3
7
14
2
13
9
5
12
17

Place your reward sticker here

Numbers everywhere

Number **one**, number **two**,
is there a number on your shoe?

Number **three**, number **four**,
what's the number on your door?

Look around you. Can you see any numbers?
Write the numbers on the line.

....

What's your shoe size? ....

What's your house number? ....

Find the missing number sticker for the phone.

Write your phone number here:

....

Place your reward sticker here

Tick tock

Numbers tell us what time it is.
Find the missing number sticker for the clock.
What time is it?

Place your sticker here

Place your reward sticker here

Happy birthday to you!

Numbers tell you when it is your birthday.
Find the missing number sticker.
Find the day of your birthday on this calendar.
Colour in the square. How old are you now?
How old will you be on your next birthday?

1	2	3	4	5
6	7	8	9	10
11	12	13	14	15
16	17	18	Place your sticker here	20
21	22	23	24	25
26	27	28	29	30
31				

11 12 13 14 15 16 17 18 19 20

Place your reward sticker here

Money

Look at these coins.

Can you draw them in order in the circles?
Start with the coin worth the smallest amount.

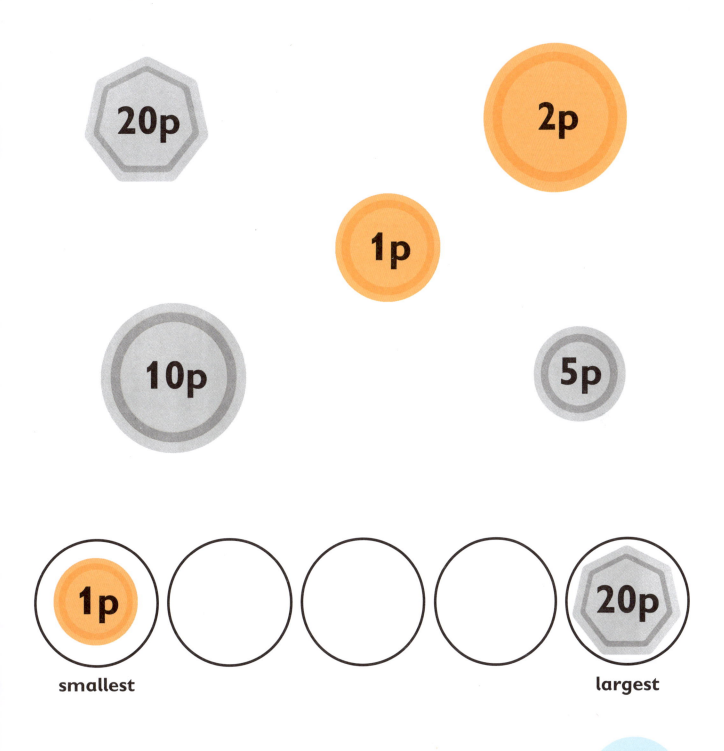

Big and small numbers

Numbers big and numbers small, show me that you know them all!

What's the **smallest** number you know? ....

What's the **largest** number you know? ....

What's your favourite number? ....

Number machine

The fun number machine has made some numbers. Write the numbers from smallest to largest in the squares.

Millions and billions!

These are huge, enormous, gigantic numbers. They are bigger than you can count.

Just imagine the millions of stars that are in the sky!

Find a sticker with a huge, enormous, gigantic number.

Place your sticker here

This is how we write **one million**.

Place your reward sticker here

Number dot-to-dot

Start at number **1** and join the numbered dots in order.

How many dots are there?

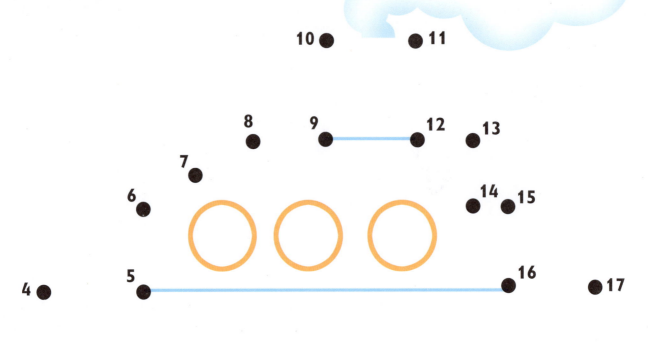

Well done! You're a star for finishing this book!

Place your reward sticker here